# THE JPS B'NAI MITZVAH TORAH COMMENTARY

**Va-yakhel** (Exodus 35:1–38:20)
Haftarah (1 Kings 7:40–50)

Rabbi Jeffrey K. Salkin

The Jewish Publication Society · Philadelphia
University of Nebraska Press · Lincoln

# INTRODUCTION

News flash: the most important thing about becoming bar or bat mitzvah isn't the party. Nor is it the presents. Nor even being able to celebrate with your family and friends—as wonderful as those things are. Nor is it even standing before the congregation and reading the prayers of the liturgy—as important as that is.

No, the most important thing about becoming bar or bat mitzvah is sharing Torah with the congregation. And why is that? Because of all Jewish skills, that is the most important one.

Here is what is true about rites of passage: you can tell what a culture values by the tasks it asks its young people to perform on their way to maturity. In American culture, you become responsible for driving, responsible for voting, and yes, responsible for drinking responsibly.

In some cultures, the rite of passage toward maturity includes some kind of trial, or a test of strength. Sometimes, it is a kind of "outward bound" camping adventure. Among the Maasai tribe in Africa, it is traditional for a young person to hunt and kill a lion. In some Hispanic cultures, fifteen year-old girls celebrate the *quinceañera*, which marks their entrance into maturity.

What is Judaism's way of marking maturity? It combines both of these rites of passage: *responsibility* and *test*. You show that you are on your way to becoming a *responsible* Jewish adult through a public *test* of strength and knowledge—reading or chanting Torah, and then teaching it to the congregation.

This is the most important Jewish ritual mitzvah (commandment), and that is how you demonstrate that you are, truly, bar or bat mitzvah—old enough to be responsible for the mitzvot.

## What Is Torah?

So, what exactly is the Torah? You probably know this already, but let's review.

The Torah (teaching) consists of "the five books of Moses," sometimes also called the *chumash* (from the Hebrew word *chameish,* which means "five"), or, sometimes, the Greek word Pentateuch (which means "the five teachings").

Here are the five books of the Torah, with their common names and their Hebrew names.

› **Genesis (The beginning), which in Hebrew is Bere'shit (from the first words—"When God began to create").** Bere'shit spans the years from Creation to Joseph's death in Egypt. Many of the Bible's best stories are in Genesis: the creation story itself; Adam and Eve in the Garden of Eden; Cain and Abel; Noah and the Flood; and the tales of the Patriarchs and Matriarchs, Abraham, Isaac, Jacob, Sarah, Rebekah, Rachel, and Leah. It also includes one of the greatest pieces of world literature, the story of Joseph, which is actually the oldest complete novel in history, comprising more than one-quarter of all Genesis.

› **Exodus (Getting out), which in Hebrew is Shemot (These are the names).** Exodus begins with the story of the Israelite slavery in Egypt. It then moves to the rise of Moses as a leader, and the Israelites' liberation from slavery. After the Israelites leave Egypt, they experience the miracle of the parting of the Sea of Reeds (or "Red Sea"); the giving of the Ten Commandments at Mount Sinai; the idolatry of the Golden Calf; and the design and construction of the Tabernacle and of the ark for the original tablets of the law, which our ancestors carried with them in the desert. Exodus also includes various ethical and civil laws, such as "You shall not wrong a stranger or oppress him, for you were strangers in the land of Egypt" (22:20).

› **Leviticus (about the Levites), or, in Hebrew, Va-yikra' (And God called).** It goes into great detail about the kinds of sacrifices that the ancient Israelites brought as offerings; the laws of ritual purity; the animals that were permitted and forbidden for eating (the beginnings of the tradition of kashrut, the Jewish dietary laws); the diagnosis of various skin diseases; the ethical laws of holiness; the ritual calendar of the Jewish year; and various agricultural laws concerning the treatment of the Land of Israel. Leviticus is basically the manual of ancient Judaism.

> **Numbers (because the book begins with the census of the Israelites), or, in Hebrew, Be-midbar (In the wilderness).** The book describes the forty years of wandering in the wilderness and the various rebellions against Moses. The constant theme: "Egypt wasn't so bad. Maybe we should go back." The greatest rebellion against Moses was the negative reports of the spies about the Land of Israel, which discouraged the Israelites from wanting to move forward into the land. For that reason, the "wilderness generation" must die off before a new generation can come into maturity and finish the journey.

> **Deuteronomy (The repetition of the laws of the Torah), or, in Hebrew, Devarim (The words).** The final book of the Torah is, essentially, Moses's farewell address to the Israelites as they prepare to enter the Land of Israel. Here we find various laws that had been previously taught, though sometimes with different wording. Much of Deuteronomy contains laws that will be important to the Israelites as they enter the Land of Israel—laws concerning the establishment of a monarchy and the ethics of warfare. Perhaps the most famous passage from Deuteronomy contains the *Shema,* the declaration of God's unity and uniqueness, and the *Ve-ahavta,* which follows it. Deuteronomy ends with the death of Moses on Mount Nebo as he looks across the Jordan Valley into the land that he will not enter.

Jews read the Torah in sequence—starting with Bere'shit right after Simchat Torah in the autumn, and then finishing Devarim on the following Simchat Torah. Each Torah portion is called a parashah (division; sometimes called a *sidrah,* a place in the order of the Torah reading). The stories go around in a full circle, reminding us that we can always gain more insights and more wisdom from the Torah. This means that if you don't "get" the meaning this year, don't worry—it will come around again.

## And What Else? The Haftarah

We read or chant the Torah from the Torah scroll—the most sacred thing that a Jewish community has in its possession. The Torah is written without vowels, and the ability to read it and chant it is part of the challenge and the test.

But there is more to the synagogue reading. Every Torah reading has an accompanying haftarah reading. Haftarah means "conclusion," because there was once a time when the service actually ended with that reading. Some scholars believe that the reading of the haftarah originated at a time when non-Jewish authorities outlawed the reading of the Torah, and the Jews read the haftarah sections instead. In fact, in some synagogues, young people who become bar or bat mitzvah read very little Torah and instead read the entire haftarah portion.

The haftarah portion comes from the Nevi'im, the prophetic books, which are the second part of the Jewish Bible. It is either read or chanted from a Hebrew Bible, or maybe from a booklet or a photocopy.

The ancient sages chose the haftarah passages because their themes reminded them of the words or stories in the Torah text. Sometimes, they chose *haftarah* with special themes in honor of a festival or an upcoming festival.

Not all books in the prophetic section of the Hebrew Bible consist of prophecy. Several are historical. For example:

The book of Joshua tells the story of the conquest and settlement of Israel.

The book of Judges speaks of the period of early tribal rulers who would rise to power, usually for the purpose of uniting the tribes in war against their enemies. Some of these leaders are famous: Deborah, the great prophetess and military leader, and Samson, the biblical strong man.

The books of Samuel start with Samuel, the last judge, and then move to the creation of the Israelite monarchy under Saul and David (approximately 1000 BCE).

The books of Kings tell of the death of King David, the rise of King Solomon, and how the Israelite kingdom split into the Northern Kingdom of Israel and the Southern Kingdom of Judah (approximately 900 BCE).

And then there are the books of the prophets, those spokesmen for God whose words fired the Jewish conscience. Their names are immortal: Isaiah, Jeremiah, Ezekiel, Amos, Hosea, among others.

Someone once said: "There is no evidence of a biblical prophet ever being invited back a second time for dinner." Why? Because the prophets were tough. They had no patience for injustice, apathy, or hypocrisy. No one escaped their criticisms. Here's what they taught:

> God commands the Jews to behave decently toward one another. In fact, God cares more about basic ethics and decency than about ritual behavior.
> God chose the Jews *not* for special privileges, but for special duties to humanity.
> As bad as the Jews sometimes were, there was always the possibility that they would improve their behavior.
> As bad as things might be now, it will not always be that way. Someday, there will be universal justice and peace. Human history is moving forward toward an ultimate conclusion that some call the Messianic Age: a time of universal peace and prosperity for the Jewish people and for all the people of the world.

## Your Mission—To Teach Torah to the Congregation

On the day when you become bar or bat mitzvah, you will be reading, or chanting, Torah—in Hebrew. You will be reading, or chanting, the haftarah—in Hebrew. That is the major skill that publicly marks the becoming of bar or bat mitzvah. But, perhaps even more important than that, you need to be able to teach something about the Torah portion, and perhaps the haftarah as well.

And that is where this book comes in. It will be a very valuable resource for you, and your family, in the b'nai mitzvah process.

Here is what you will find in it:

> A brief **summary** of every Torah portion. This is a basic overview of the portion; and, while it might not refer to everything in the Torah portion, it will explain its most important aspects.
> A list of the **major ideas** in the Torah portion. The purpose: to make the Torah portion real, in ways that we can relate to. Every Torah portion contains unique ideas, and when you put all

of those ideas together, you actually come up with a list of Judaism's most important ideas.

> Two *divrei Torah* ("words of Torah," or "sermonettes") for each portion. These *divrei Torah* explain significant aspects of the Torah portion in accessible, reader-friendly language. Each *devar Torah* contains references to **traditional** Jewish sources (those that were written before the modern era), as well as **modern** sources and quotes. We have searched, far and wide, to find sources that are unusual, interesting, and not just the "same old stuff" that many people already know about the Torah portion. Why did we include these minisermons in the volume? Not because we want you to simply copy those sermons and pass them off as your own (that would be cheating), though you are free to quote from them. We included them so that you can see what is possible—how you can try to make meaning for yourself out of the words of Torah.

> **Connections:** This is perhaps the most valuable part. It's a list of questions that you can ask yourself, or that others might help you think about—any of which can lead to the creation of your *devar Torah*.

Note: you don't have to like everything that's in a particular Torah portion. Some aren't that loveable. Some are hard to understand; some are about religious practices that people today might find confusing, and even offensive; some contain ideas that we might find totally outmoded.

But this doesn't have to get in the way. After all, most kids spend a lot of time thinking about stories that contain ideas that modern people would find totally bizarre. Any good medieval fantasy story falls into that category.

And we also believe that, if you spend just a little bit of time with those texts, you can begin to understand what the author was trying to say.

This volume goes one step further. Sometimes, the haftarah comes off as a second thought, and no one really thinks about it. We have tried to solve that problem by including a **summary** of each haftarah, and then a mini-sermon on the haftarah. This will help you learn how these sacred words are relevant to today's world, and even to your own life.

All Bible quotations come from the NJPS translation, which is found in the many different editions of the JPS TANAKH; in the Conservative movement's *Etz Hayim: Torah and Commentary;* in the Reform movement's *Torah: A Modern Commentary;* and in other Bible commentaries and study guides.

### How Do I Write a *Devar Torah?*

It really is easier than it looks.

There are many ways of thinking about the *devar Torah.* It is, of course, a short sermon on the meaning of the Torah (and, perhaps, the haftarah) portion. It might even be helpful to think of the *devar Torah* as a "book report" on the portion itself.

The most important thing you can know about this sacred task is: *Learn* the words. *Love* the words. Teach people what it could mean to *live* the words.

Here's a basic outline for a *devar Torah:*

"My Torah portion is (name of portion) _____ ,
   from the book of _____ , chapter

   _____ .

"In my Torah portion, we learn that _____
   (Summary of portion)

"For me, the most important lesson of this Torah portion is (what
   is the best thing in the portion? Take the portion as a whole;
   your *devar Torah* does not have to be only, or specifically, on the
   verses that you are reading).

"As I learned my Torah portion, I found myself wondering:
> *Raise a question that the Torah portion itself raises.*
> *"Pick a fight"* with the portion. Argue with it.
> *Answer a question* that is listed in the "Connections" section of
   each Torah portion.
> *Suggest a question to your rabbi* that you would want the rabbi
   to answer in his or her own *devar Torah* or sermon.

"I have lived the values of the Torah by _____
(here, you can talk about how the Torah portion relates to your own life. If you have done a mitzvah project, you can talk about that here).

## How To Keep It from Being Boring (and You from Being Bored)

Some people just don't like giving traditional speeches. From our perspective, that's really okay. Perhaps you can teach Torah in a different way—one that makes sense to you.

> ‣ Write an "open letter" to one of the characters in your Torah portion. "Dear Abraham: I hope that your trip to Canaan was not too hard . . ." "Dear Moses: Were you afraid when you got the Ten Commandments on Mount Sinai? I sure would have been . . ."
> ‣ Write a news story about what happens. Imagine yourself to be a television or news reporter. "Residents of neighboring cities were horrified yesterday as the wicked cities of Sodom and Gomorrah were burned to the ground. Some say that God was responsible . . ."
> ‣ Write an imaginary interview with a character in your Torah portion.
> ‣ Tell the story from the point of view of another character, or a minor character, in the story. For instance, tell the story of the Garden of Eden from the point of view of the serpent. Or the story of the Binding of Isaac from the point of view of the ram, which was substituted for Isaac as a sacrifice. Or perhaps the story of the sale of Joseph from the point of view of his coat, which was stripped off him and dipped in a goat's blood.
> ‣ Write a poem about your Torah portion.
> ‣ Write a song about your Torah portion.
> ‣ Write a play about your Torah portion, and have some friends act it out with you.
> ‣ Create a piece of artwork about your Torah portion.

The bottom line is: Make this a joyful experience. Yes—it could even be fun.

### The Very Last Thing You Need to Know at This Point

The Torah scroll is written without vowels. Why? Don't *sofrim* (Torah scribes) know the vowels?

Of course they do.

So, why do they leave the vowels out?

One reason is that the Torah came into existence at a time when sages were still arguing about the proper vowels, and the proper pronunciation.

But here is another reason: The Torah text, as we have it today, and as it sits in the scroll, is actually *an unfinished work*. Think of it: the words are just sitting there. Because they have no vowels, it is as if they have no voice.

When we read the Torah publicly, we give voice to the ancient words. And when we find meaning in those ancient words, and we talk about those meanings, those words jump to life. They enter our lives. They make our world deeper and better.

Mazal tov to you, and your family. This is your journey toward Jewish maturity. Love it.

# THE TORAH

❖ Va-yakhel: Exodus 35:1–38:20

Parashat Terumah gave the instructions for the design of the Tabernacle, and Va-yakhel now follows through on those plans.

It emphasizes that the Israelites enthusiastically (we might even say
too enthusiastically!) brought the materials for the building of the Tabernacle. The text singles out two Israelites, Bezalel and Oholiab, as the
master craftsmen whose work went into the Tabernacle's construction.

## Summary

- Moses expands upon the earlier commandment regarding Shabbat, as found in the Ten Commandments. Whoever does any work shall be put to death, and kindling fire is considered a violation of Shabbat. (35:1–3)
- Moses reminds the Israelites that they should bring donations for the construction of the Tabernacle, and he gives specific instructions about the materials. Moses's directions emphasize the role of the heart: gifts must come from "everyone whose heart so moves him" and those who are skilled (*chakham lev,* "wise of heart") should be involved in the project. There is a particular role for women as well—as spinners and weavers. (35:4–29)
- Moses showcases the talent of Bezalel and Oholiab, who are the master craftsmen of the Tabernacle. (35:30–35)
- The people bring an overabundance of gifts to the building of the Tabernacle, and their gift giving has to be stopped. (36:5–6)

## The Big Ideas

> **The building of the Tabernacle might have been an act of atonement for having built the Golden Calf.** It follows right after the building of the calf, and some commentators believe the purpose of the Tabernacle is for God to demonstrate that the Divine Presence is still in the midst of the people and that they need not resort to an idol.

> **Shabbat and the construction of the Tabernacle seem to be linked together.** It is hardly an accident that the observance of Shabbat is mentioned in the same breath as the design of the Tabernacle. When later generations of sages tried to figure out exactly what kind of work would be prohibited on Shabbat, they decided that any kind of labor that was involved in the building of the Tabernacle would be a violation of Shabbat.

> **While the building of the Tabernacle is a mitzvah, the Israelites must contribute to its building with willing hearts.** It is not enough for God to simply demand that the Israelites do something. Their emotions have to be involved. They have to feel connected to what was going on. The text makes it clear that everyone was involved in some way. The building of the Tabernacle symbolizes the unity of the Jewish people.

> **Judaism believes that there should be sacred roles for artists and craftspeople.** Because Jews and Judaism are often associated with words and abstract thinking, it is important to remember the gifts of those who are artistically inclined and those who work with their hands. Israel's most prominent arts academy, the Bezalel Academy of Arts and Design, in Jerusalem, is named for one of the Jewish people's ancient craftsmen. It is also significant that Bezalel is from the tribe of Judah (the most powerful tribe) and Oholiab is from the tribe of Dan (the weakest tribe). In the building of the Tabernacle, the strong and the weak work together.

> **The people actually brought too much to the building of the Tabernacle.** While this would probably be every Jewish leader's greatest dream, it teaches us that too much enthusiasm for a project—even a sacred project—could become dangerous.

*Divrei Torah*

STOP GIVING—PLEASE!

Here's the scene: You are raising money for your youth group or your sports team. It starts with people giving you a dollar or two, and then people start coming back and giving you five dollars, then twenty dollars, then fifty dollars. You cannot believe all the money that is coming in! You start to get uneasy and at some point even begin to wish that people would just stop already.

Hard to imagine, right? What would be wrong with all that money coming in? That people might go nuts giving? That people might get competitive with each other?

That is exactly what happens in the Torah portion. There is a collection of materials for the building of the Tabernacle. The people keep giving and giving, but at a certain point Moses says that they bring too much. The artisans who are getting the materials protest that there's no room for everything. Moses tells the people to stop bringing those precious materials.

But why do they go overboard? After all, think of the last time this happened. The Israelites had been equally enthusiastic in bringing their donations to the building of the Golden Calf.

Now it could be that the Israelites decide that the way to make up for the sin of the Golden Calf is to use their energies to do something better. In the words of Bible scholar Nehama Leibowitz: "They made amends with the very same thing with which they had sinned. It was their gold earrings that gilded the calf and again their 'earrings and every kind of gold ornaments' that they contributed to the Tabernacle."

There is another major difference besides the ultimate destination of the gifts. When the people brought donations of gold to the building of the Golden Calf, they just deposited their donations. The Torah doesn't say anything about how the people felt about what they were doing. On the other hand, the building of the Tabernacle explicitly calls for a willing heart. As the medieval commentator Isaac Abravanel teaches: "for the sake of the Lord and not for any other motive." So what could be bad about all this enthusiastic giving? Interesting:

in Jewish law you are not supposed to give too much *tzedakah* (charity), lest you put yourself in a shaky financial position. You are supposed to be generous, but not go overboard (most often defined as giving away more than 20 percent of your income).

The bottom line: there are limits to everything. By all means, give charity. Support worthy causes. But make sure that you don't turn it into too much of a good thing. The making of the Tabernacle calls for self-discipline—like most things in life.

### THE WORK OF OUR HANDS

One of the greatest educational institutions in the State of Israel is the Bezalel Academy of Arts and Design, in Jerusalem. Some of the most creative people in the Jewish world have studied there. The origin of the name comes from this week's Torah portion, where we learn that Bezalel was the chief artisan of the ancient Tabernacle. (Note: Bezalel had a colleague, Oholiab. But there is no Oholiab Academy in Jerusalem.) All that those art and design students probably know about Bezalel is that he was the boss.

Who could blame them? Frankly, the Bible doesn't have that much else to say about Bezalel. We know the name of his father—Uri. Was Bezalel married? Did he have children? Was he gifted as a child? Who did he study with? We don't know. Bible scholar Avivah Zornberg writes: "Just as the Golden Calf emerged suddenly from the flames, so did Bezalel's talent. He enters the world without explanation."

Yet Bezalel's talent is nothing short of miraculous. How could he have learned his great skill? Certainly not in Egypt! The medieval sage Nachmanides teaches: "When Israel was in Egypt, they were crushed under the work of mortar and brick, and they had acquired no knowledge of how to work in silver and gold. It was therefore a wonder that there could be found among them someone as skillful as Bezalel. For even among those who study from experts, you cannot find one who is proficient in all these crafts."

No wonder that the biblical text says that Bezalel was filled with "skill, ability, and knowledge" (35:31). It was the only way that he could have pulled off such a wonderful artistic feat.

What do we learn from Bezalel? Judaism is not just about books and studying; it is also about the creative arts. Starting in the Middle Ages, there were beautiful *Haggadot* and illuminated manuscripts. Today, there is more creativity in Jewish ritual objects than at almost any time in history. Just go to any Judaica store or Jewish museum and you will see beautiful synagogue art, Kiddush cups, *tallitot, mezuzot, Havdalah* sets, *etrog* boxes, seder plates, and more. Sure—you can make *Kiddush* with a paper cup, but why should you? Judaism teaches the concept of *hiddur mitzvah,* that you should adorn or beautify a mitzvah whenever you can.

At the founding ceremonies of the Bezalel school, the first chief rabbi of prestate Israel, Rabbi Abraham Kook, said: "The desire for the beginnings of an art institution in the Land of Israel is in essence a sign of life, a sign of hope, salvation and comfort. Our nation looks well upon the sweet beauty of art which is expressed through human creativity." Let's remember the artists who have enriched Jewish life in our time by the wonderful work that they do. And if you have skills like that, put them to work for the Jewish people.

Connections

› What things do you think that modern Jews should not do on Shabbat?

› In what things do you invest your heart? In other words, what are those things that move your heart, and that you want to excel in?

› What skills do you have? How have you made them work for Judaism?

› A midrash says that Bezalel was thirteen years old when he built the Tabernacle. Why do you think the ancient sages assigned that age to that great feat? What might this have to do with thirteen being the age of bar and bat mitzvah?

› Can you think of times when people have become overenthusiastic in doing a good thing?

# THE HAFTARAH

### ❖ Va-yakhel: 1 Kings 7:40–50

Despite the fact that the second book of the Torah is called Exodus (or, in Hebrew, Shemot, "Names"), the greatest number of words in the book of Exodus is devoted, not to names, but to the construction of the ancient Tabernacle (the *mishkan*). It's not because religious buildings are the most important thing in the world; it's because those buildings make community possible. That is why there are several *haftarah* about the construction of the ancient Temple in Jerusalem, which was the successor to the desert Tabernacle and King Solomon's biggest project.

In this haftarah, we meet a talented bronze worker named Hiram (in Hebrew, Hirom). (That name may sound familiar to you, but he's not to be confused with Hiram in Haftarat Terumah, who is King Hiram of Tyre, a city-state in modern-day Lebanon, who helped King Solomon build the ancient Temple.)

In this haftarah, we read about Hiram the artisan. His bronze contributions were so heavy that King Solomon could not weigh them. We also read about the gold furnishings that Solomon made for the Temple: altar, candelabra, basins, ladles, and doors. All these details of the Temple parallel the description of the Tabernacle.

### Call Me Hiram/Hirom

How many ways can you spell the name Deborah. Yes, there's Deborah—or is it spelled Debra? And her nickname: Debbie, or Debbi, or Debi, or Debby?

The same thing is true with Hiram. It's spelled two different ways in Hebrew. So sometimes it is more like Hirom. To make matters worse, there are two different people with the two variations of the same name!

First, as mentioned above, there is King Hiram of Tyre, who helped King Solomon build the ancient Temple in Jerusalem. And now, in this haftarah, we read of another person with the same name, and he also helped with the building of the ancient Temple.

King Hiram was mostly involved in sending building materials—notably, those majestic trees known as the cedars of Lebanon—to Solomon to use in the construction of the Temple. This other Hiram is involved in the same project but from a different angle. He is a talented bronze worker. It seems that his major talent is in crafting huge, rounded pieces made of bronze. He comes from Tyre, like King Hiram. But he definitely is not a king, because he does not come from anything resembling royal lineage. We read that Hiram's father was a craftsman of Tyre, and that his mother was a widow of the tribe of Naphtali. That would make him half-Israelite on his mother's side. Whether he considered himself Jewish is unclear, since in those days lineage passed from the father.

Shall we imagine a backstory for this "new" Hiram? Where did he come from? How did he get his name? How did he learn his trade?

As I have written: "It would start with a nameless Israelite widow. She meets a nameless Tyrian craftsman, and they fall in love. She gives birth to an infant whom she names Hiram, and, as fathers will often do, his father teaches him everything he knows about metalworking and other kinds of craftsmanship." As for Hiram's mother, perhaps she also taught him things. Perhaps she taught him of her own people—their stories, dreams, and songs.

And so, Hiram became a craftsman. A rather good craftsman. Perhaps the actions of his royal namesake had inspired him, and he willingly and enthusiastically made the trip to Jerusalem to become part of the holy process of building the Temple. Perhaps—just perhaps—Solomon's request sparked something inside this Hiram's soul, just like the spark in the king that led to his collaboration with Solomon. True, he had not been raised in the Land of Israel. True, he had been cut off from his people. But he knew one thing: when Solomon called him, he wanted to help.

Rabbi W. Gunther Plaut writes: "In the Torah, God chose Bezalel to do the work on the Tabernacle; in the haftarah, Solomon chose Hiram to help." I wonder what Solomon thought of the coincidence that the king and the key craftsman had (almost) the same name. Maybe it wasn't just a coincidence . . .

❖ Notes

❖ Notes

CPSIA information can be obtained
at www.ICGtesting.com
Printed in the USA
LVHW08s0951050818
585984LV00004B/437/P